Provincetown

The Delaplaine Long Weekend Guide

TABLE OF CONTENTS

Chapter 1 – WHY P'TOWN? P - 4

Chapter 2 – GETTING ABOUT – 11

Chapter 3 – WHERE TO STAY – 15

Chapter 4 – WHERE TO EAT – 27

Chapter 5 – WHAT TO SEE & DO – 42

Chapter 6 – NIGHTLIFE – 54

Chapter 7 – SHOPPING & SERVICES – 59

INDEX – 64

OTHER BOOKS BY THE AUTHOR – 68

Chapter 1
WHY P'TOWN?

Every time I'm in the Hamptons, the thought crosses my mind that "I'd rather be in P'town."

Every time I'm on Cape Cod, I think two things: "Thank God it never turned into the Hamptons" and "Thank God it's still the same."

PROVINCETOWN
The Delaplaine 2021 Long Weekend Guide

Andrew Delaplaine

NO BUSINESS HAS PAID A SINGLE PENNY OR GIVEN _ANYTHING_ TO BE INCLUDED IN THIS BOOK.

GET 3 FREE NOVELS
Like political thrillers?
See next page to download 3 great page-turners—
FREE - no strings attached.

Senior Editors - *Renee & Sophie Delaplaine*
Senior Writer - **James Cubby**

Cover Photo by Mark Martins from Pixbay
Copyright © by Gramercy Park Press - All rights reserved.

WANT 3 FREE THRILLERS?

Why, of course you do!

If you like these writers--
Vince Flynn, Brad Thor, Tom Clancy, James Patterson, David Baldacci, John Grisham, Brad Meltzer, Daniel Silva, Don DeLillo

If you like these TV series –
House of Cards, Scandal, West Wing, The Good Wife, Madam Secretary, Designated Survivor

> You'll love the **unputdownable** series about Jack Houston St. Clair, with political intrigue, romance, and loads of action and suspense.

Besides writing travel books, I've written political thrillers for many years that have delighted hundreds of thousands of readers. I want to introduce you to my work!
Send me an email and I'll send you a link where you can download the first 3 books in my bestselling series, absolutely FREE.

Mention **this book** when you email me.
andrewdelaplaine@mac.com

It's not of course. Nothing ever really is the same. But when you run into old-timers on Long Island, they'll tell you how it was in the Hamptons before the mega-rich moved in and built their monstrously inappropriate mansions, bringing along with them, naturally, their monstrously inappropriate attitudes. The Hamptons with their fancy shops and nightclubs. (Can you ever imagine a NIGHTCLUB on Cape Cod? Not really. Who would ever go to it? I'm not including P'town in this statement—with all the gay people out there, of course they have nightclubs.)

Cape Cod is really one of the great things about America. There's a unique ecosystem or lifestyle or way of life or mindset on the Cape, however you may want to describe it.

The cheesy little stores selling dust collecting souvenirs, the roadside seafood shacks selling fried clams the way they have for decades, the quiet beaches on Nantucket Bay, the shops selling saltwater taffy and other summer goodies—all of it is remarkably the same as it was when my grandmother used to drag us out there from Boston every summer.

It's kinda like the northern version of the Florida Keys. (Though the local people couldn't be more different if they tried—the ones up on the Cape actually read books and know who's President. In the Keys, they couldn't care less.)

Like Key West, Cape Cod, and especially P'town, has been a magnate for artists of every type. If you're lucky, you might be able to catch filmmaker John Waters tooling around town on his weird looking bike.

Just as the Keys are divided into three parts, the Upper, Middle and Lower Keys, Cape Cod goes them one better and is divided roughly into four parts: the Upper Cape, Mid-Cape, Lower Cape and Outer Cape. (Five parts if you count the Islands—Martha's Vineyard, Nantucket and Gosnold.)

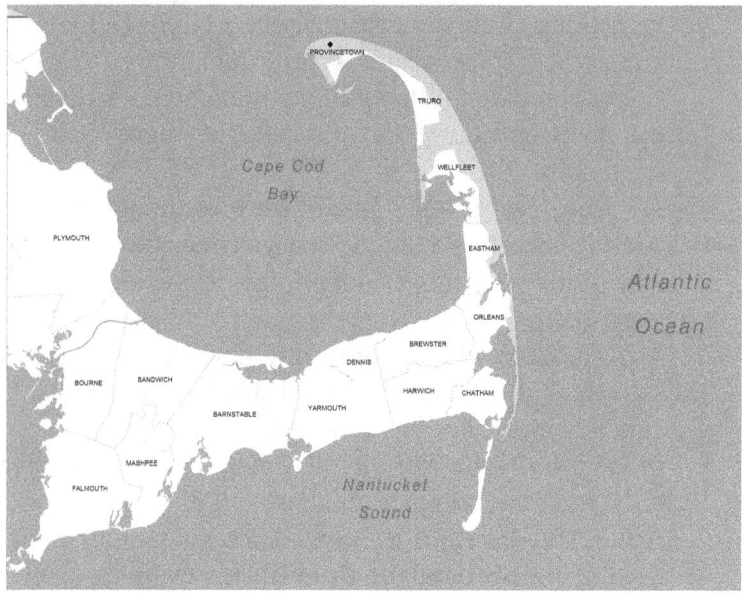

UPPER CAPE

The Upper Cape runs north to south and is bounded by Buzzards Bay and the Cape Cod Canal. Sandwich takes the honors as the oldest town on the Cape, thus the most historic. Charming Falmouth and its lovely waterfront aren't far away. Wood's Hole, of course, is home to the big oceanographic institute you've probably heard a lot about over the years. Then there's Mashpee, New Seabury, Bourne.

MID-CAPE

Exactly as the name indicates, Mid-Cape is in the middle of the peninsula, boasting towns like Hyannis (famed for its Kennedy connection), Osterville (where we stayed with grandmother in a whitewashed house), Barnstable Village, Dennis, Yarmouthport, Centerville, West Barnstable, Craigville, Cummaquid, HyannisPort.

LOWER CAPE

In the geography of the "arm" that Cape Cod forms, this area starts at the elbow and makes its way north. Chatham is the jewel of the Lower Cape, sporting a charmingly quaint downtown area, shops and restaurants. Chatham makes a great place to stay because it's so centrally located to the rest of Cape Cod. Here you'll find Also in the Lower Cape is Orleans, claimed to be the spot where Leif Eriksson landed in 1003. (Long before the lobster roll, he probably had his lobster cooked over a spit with no drawn butter and loved them just as much as we do today.) Also here you'll find Harwichport and Brewster.

The thing that gets me about Leif Eriksson is why in God's name he didn't send his boat back and tell the crew to bring their families. Think of the real estate he could have stolen from the Indians.

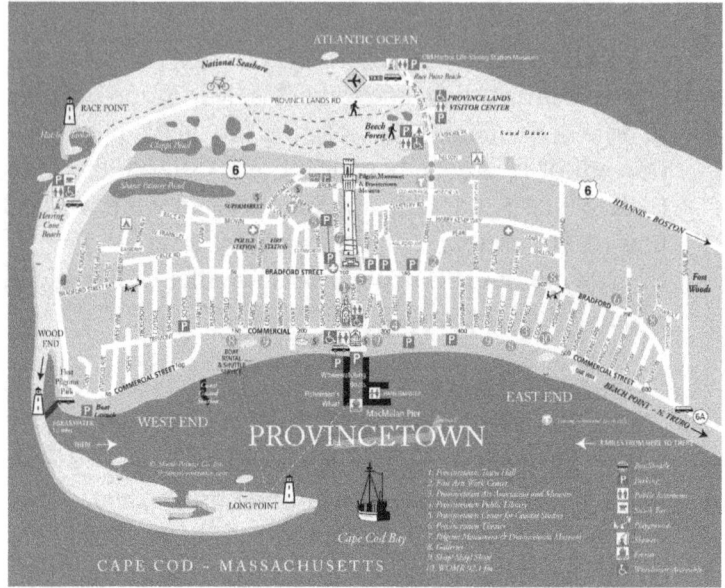

OUTER CAPE

As the "forearm" of Cape Cod moves north, you enter what is called the Outer Cape. On one side you have Cape Cod Bay and on the other the Atlantic. The peninsula becomes quite narrow out here, and you pass through towns like Eastham (not that there's much of a "town" there) and Truro with great views from the cliffs and the Cape Code Light, before you get to wonderful Wellfleet. (Think "Wellfleet oysters.") This is a great little town I love very much, a civilized respite from the madness of the last stop, Provincetown, or "P'town" to locals, a sizeable number of whom are gay.

P'town is a world unto its own on Cape Cod. There are dozens of little towns on the Cape you could pick up, move 20 or 30 miles and set down again and nobody would notice anything different.

But you couldn't do that with P'town. It's completely unique.

THE ISLANDS
Martha's Vineyard & Nantucket

Several Cape Cod harbors have ferries that will take you to Martha's Vineyard.

The **Island Queen** operates out of Falmouth Harbor. Quickest way if you don't have a car. 30-40 minutes from dock to dock. 75 Falmouth Heights Rd, 508-548-4800. www.islandqueen.com/
Steamship Authority takes cars over. Must reserve a place for your car. 1 Cowdry Rd, Wood's Hole, and also from 65 South St, Hyannis. 508-495-3278 for people reservations, 508-477-8600 to reserve a place for your car. www.steamshipauthority.com/

Pied Piper, 278 Scranton Ave, Falmouth, 508-548-9400. www.falmouthedgartownferry.com/ Offers only service to Edgartown in the summer aboard a 72-foot vessel.

Hy-Line Cruises
220 Ocean St, Hyannis, 800-492-8082
hylinecruises.com/
Serves both islands

WHEN TO VISIT

I prefer the slightly off-season Spring and Autumn periods over the high summer season to visit Cape Cod. But then, I can do without most beach activities that if you have a family, you'll want to take advantage of. Kids want to swim. The worst time for me is 4th of July through Labor Day. This is the high summer season. The four weeks before or the four weeks after make the perfect time to visit. The crowds are less, the rates are lower, you can get into the best restaurants without a hassle and the car traffic is reduced to somewhat sane levels, not something you can say in high season.

Chapter 2
GETTING ABOUT

You'll only need a car if you plan to travel around the Cape. In P'town itself, you can grab a taxi and go anywhere in town for about $5.

Otherwise, use bikes.

GALE FORCE BEACH MARKET & BIKE RENTALS
144 Bradford St Ext, Provincetown, 508–487–4849
www.galeforcebikes.com

PTOWN BIKES
www.ptownbikes.com
42 Bradford St, Provincetown, 508-487-8735
They'll have what you need. Various packages.

AIR SERVICE
From Boston, you can fly on **Cape Air**. Flight takes about 20 minutes. Details at: www.capeair.com

FERRY SERVICE
From Boston, you can also take the ferry. Details at www.mafastferry.com - takes about 90 minutes.

BUS SERVICE
There is bus service along the Cape direct from Logan Airport in Boston. Details at www.p-b.com.

Chapter 3
WHERE TO STAY

DID YOU FIND AN INTERESTING PLACE?
If you discover a place you think I should check out on my next visit, drop me a line, will you? I'll mention your name if I end up listing it.
andrewdelaplaine@mac.com

Bungalows

An old song has this lyric: "In a cozy bungalow, we'd know such sweet delight." From one end of the Cape to the other you'll find hundreds of these bungalows, cottages, what-have-you. While they are quaint and look great, if you want the bungalow experience, be sure you choose carefully. Once you go into some of these little houses, you see how awful so many of them can be. Another thing: lots of places are not open all year.

BRASS KEY GUESTHOUSE
67 Bradford St, Provincetown, 508-487-9005
www.brasskey.com
Across the street and down a bit from the **Crown Pointe** is this little upmarket complex of 9 restored historic buildings, a pool and gardens. Some rooms

have fireplaces and whirlpools. Nice bar, the **Shipwreck Lounge**, where I've found myself wrecked a few times too many. On-site Spa as well. Lively crowd (mostly gay).

CAPE COLONY INN
280 Bradford St., Provincetown, 508-487-1755/ 800-841-6716
www.capecolonyinn.com
This Inn is standard, has everything you need. The décor and furniture is simple but modern. The photographs featured in each room is a nice touch. Each photograph is unique to the room by independent photographers who captured the local scenery. The Inn has had some renovations so the bathrooms and common areas are up-to-date. There is a dog friendly public beach 2 blocks away. They have free continental breakfast, Keurig Brewing machine, iPod alarm clock radios, parking, and free wifi.

THE CAPTAIN'S HOUSE
350A Commercial St., Provincetown, 508-487-9353
www.captainshouseptown.com
There are 12 rooms, 3 on the first floor with private bathrooms and 9 on the second with shared bathrooms. They are small but classic. Each room has its own air conditioner. There is a relaxing private deck., continental breakfast, and free wifi. They have been working on some improvements such as the living room.

CARPE DIEM GUESTHOUSE & SPA
12-14 Johnson St., Provincetown, 508-487-4242/

800-487-0132
www.carpediemguesthouse.com
There are 7 classic rooms with private bathrooms, 8 deluxe rooms with fireplaces, and 3 suites with fireplaces and whirlpool tubs. The names of the

rooms are dedicated to poets who seized the day in Provincetown. They have a German-style breakfast and a daily wine happy hour. There is the Namaste Spa where you can relax and experience the benefits of heat, steam, touch and aromas. No smoking and no pets.

CREW'S QUARTERS
198 Commercial St., Provincetown, 508-487-5900
www.crewsquartersptown.com
This is a guesthouse for gay guys and their friends, formerly know as the Ranch. Small rooms with 3 shared bathrooms. There is no tv or air conditioner but they do have wifi.

CROWN & ANCHOR INN
247 Commercial St., Provincetown, 508-487-1430
www.onlyatthecrown.com
Centrally located, they have 18 rooms and luxury suites available. If you're a party person, then this is the place to stay. They have a nightclub (**Paramount**), video bar (**Wave Video Bar**), a cabaret venue, poolside bar with a heated pool, and a leather bar (**The Vault**). They also have a restaurant named the **Central House Restaurant**.

CROWNE POINTE
82 Bradford St, Provincetown, 508-413-6022
www.crownepointe.com
Across the street and down a bit from the **BRASS KEY GUESTHOUSE** is this complex centered around a 19th Century house featuring pool and gardens. You've got 6 historic buildings here lovingly

restored. Can't get a better location in P'town. Hardwood floors, tasteful décor. Afternoon tea as well as free wine and cheese prior to dinner. Their restaurant is **The Pointe**, an intimate place (only 50 seats) in the old captain's mansion. Menu highlights: locally caught fish, bacon & deviled eggs, poached lobster & chive gnocchi, tuna tartare & caviar. On site **Shui Spa** is full-service. No kids under 16 (this is a romantic getaway, remember?), but they have one room that they'll let pets stay in.

FOXBERRY INN
29 Bradford Street Extension, Provincetown, 508-487-8583
www.thefoxberryinn.com
They are 1 mile from the center square or the Herring Cove. They have 12 refurbished rooms, some with ocean view. They have an extended continental breakfast and afternoon tea with refreshments. There is parking on the premises and free shuttle service to and from the airport.

THE GASLAMP BED & BREAKFAST
97 Bradford St., Provincetown, 508-487-6636/ 877-697-6636
www.thegaslampptown.com
Located in the center of P'town where you are close to shops, bars and clubs, this Victorian gem has a spacious backyard deck where clothing is optional. They have a hot tub where you can unwind. All the rooms have a/c and range in size with the largest one big enough for 6 guests. Some rooms have private baths and the rest semi-private.

GIFFORD HOUSE
9 Carver St., Provincetown, 508-487-0688/ 800-434-0130
www.giffordhouse.com
This is one of the original historic hotels in P'town with a restaurant, cocktail lounge, bar and piano bar.

They have double rooms or two bedroom suites with water views. From some of the rooms you can see the Pilgrim Monument. 2/3 of their guest rooms are air conditioned. Free continental breakfast.

LAND'S END INN
22 Commercial St., Provincetown, 508-487-0706
www.landsendinn.com
I like this Inn because of the décor and amazing views, There are 18 beautiful rooms. Great for weddings. Pet friendly.

PRINCE ALBERT GUEST HOUSE
164-166 Commercial St., Provincetown, 508-487-1850
www.PrinceAlbertGuestHouse.com
The guesthouse was created by joining together the historic 19th century homes of 2 sea captains, making up 18 rooms with private baths. Modern amenities. Great views with oversized bay windows with beautiful water views. They have landscaped gardens, large hot tub, private sunning patios, wifi, and 2 computer work stations.

THE RED INN
15 Commercial St, Provincetown, 508-487-7334
www.theredinn.com
Right on Provincetown Harbor you'll find excellent lodgings in an inn that's been here since 1915. Tasteful décor, fireplaces, beamed ceilings, wide-

planked pine flooring. They have 3 nicely appointed guest rooms, 3 large suites and 2 luxury residences, all with drop-dead views of the harbor and bay. The restaurant here is also good: pan roasted local cod on a bed of rosemary potatoes and applewood bacon. The lamb chops are tops as well. The bar here makes a great place to grab a drink and absorb the atmosphere, or even better, enjoy the sunset.

ROSE ACRE
5 Center St., Provincetown, 508-487-2347
www.roseacreguests.com
This is an 1840 house tucked away on a private drive in the center of town. It was once the house of a Portuguese fishing family. The lodgings consist of the Garden Cottage, Studio, the Asian Studio, and the Penthouse which is a five room suite. There is parking on site, private entrances and baths, full kitchens, wifi, a/c, gas grill, beach towels, umbrellas, and chairs.

SANDCASTLE RESORT & CLUB
929 Commercial St., Provincetown, 508-487-9300
www.sandcastlecapecod.com
One of the largest resort complexes in P'town, 200 feet of private sandy beach with great views over the bay and waterfront. They have available about 140 different types of units from 1 bedroom suites and studios, to motel rooms. They have a ton of activities. There is an indoor pool and outdoor pool, Jacuzzi, fitness center, poolside grill, picnic areas, tennis, basketball, beach volleyball, table tennis, horseshoes, and shuffleboard.

SURFSIDE HOTEL AND SUITES
543 Commercial St., Provincetown, 508-487-1726/
800-421-1726
www.surfsideinn.cc
Open seasonally from April through October, they have redecorated rooms with many amenities such as microwave, refrigerator, cable, balcony, and bathrobes. They are pet friendly with a fee. You have access to their private beach and poolside bar service.

WHITE PORCH INN
7 Johnson St., Provincetown, 508-364-2549
www.whiteporchinn.com
This art hotel has 9 rooms highlighting contemporary art. The rooms in the main house and the carriage house have private baths, flat screen TVs with DVD players, audio systems with MP3 connectivity, free wifi, a/c, and original paintings by artists from around the world. Many of the rooms also include fireplaces and spa tubs.

Chapter 4
WHERE TO EAT

DID YOU FIND AN INTERESTING PLACE?
If you discover a place you think I should check out on my next visit, drop me a line, will you? I'll mention your name if I end up listing it.
andrewdelaplaine@mac.com

ARNOLD'S LOBSTER & CLAM BAR
3580 State Hwy, Eastham, 508-255-2575
www.arnoldsrestaurant.com
CUISINE: Seafood, Ice cream and frozen yogurt
DRINKS: Full Bar
SERVING: 11:30 am – 9:30pm daily

PRICE RANGE: $$
Since 1976 they've been serving a fried lobster tail that consistently draws raves.

BAYSIDE BETSY'S
177 Commercial St., Provincetown, 508-487-6566
www.baysidebetsys.com
CUISINE: Seafood, American (Traditional)
DRINKS: Full Bar
SERVING: Daily breakfast, lunch, and dinner
PRICE RANGE: $$
They open off-season for breakfast, lunch, and dinner. It is casual fine waterfront dining. Great for breakfast. Ask for their specials of the day.

BUBALA'S BY THE BAY
185 Commercial St., Provincetown, 508-487-0773
www.bubalas.com
CUISINE: American (New)
DRINKS: Full Bar

SERVING: Daily brunch, lunch, and dinner
PRICE RANGE: $$
Closes in winter. Great to sit back and people watch while enjoying your meal outside in their patio area. Roasted oysters, Caribbean crab cakes, roasted duck quesadilla, roasted whole flounder de-boned. They also have indoor seating if you prefer. There's usually some form of live entertainment.

THE CANTEEN
225 Commercial St, Provincetown, 508-487-3800
www.thecanteenptown.com
CUISINE: Seafood/Fish & Chips
DRINKS: Beer & Wine Only
SERVING: Lunch, Dinner; closed Mon, Tues, & Wed
PRICE RANGE: $$
A popular eatery of locals and tourists features a great menu of seafood and sandwiches. Favorites include Oyster po'boy sandwich and Clam chowder.

CIRO & SAL'S
4 Kiley Ct, Provincetown, 508-487-6444
www.ciroandsals.com
CUISINE: Italian, Seafood
DRINKS: Full Bar
SERVING: Dinner
PRICE RANGE: $$$
This go-to eatery for Northern Italian cuisine attracts fans year-round. Favorites include: Breaded veal cutlet served with spaghetti and Oven roasted salmon with a shrimp reduction sauce over risotto. Great wine cellar.

FANIZZI'S BY THE SEA
539 Commercial St., Provincetown, 508-487-1964
www.fanizzisrestaurant.com
CUISINE: American (New), Seafood; Italian
DRINKS: Full Bar
SERVING: Daily lunch and dinner; year-round
PRICE RANGE: $$
The perk of eating here is the magnificent water views. It's not only right on the water, it's *over* the water, jutting out over the bay. Besides the Italian specialties, they have lots of seafood, but the best dishes combine the two; Cajun Seafood Alfredo, for instance. Or get the excellent tortellini carbonara and add a juicy lobster tail for a few dollars more and you've got one hell of a dish.

FRONT STREET
230 Commercial St, Provincetown, 508-487-9715
www.frontstreetrestaurant.com
CUISINE: Italian
DRINKS: Full Bar
SERVING: Dinner
PRICE RANGE: $$$

Kathy & Donna are the owners here in this lovely eatery situated on the ground floor of a Victorian mansion. Italy and southern France are the culinary inspirations behind the food here. Amarone roasted boneless beef short rib, truffled Sachetti alla Carbonara, eggplant Involtini, Italian sausage with polenta, lots of great pasta creations.

JOHN DOUGH'S
258 Commercial St, Provincetown, 508-487-7776
No Website
CUISINE: Pizza, Sushi
DRINKS: Full Bar
SERVING: Lunch and dinner
PRICE RANGE: $$
This is the place to go if you and your partner can't make up your mind whether you want sushi or in the

mood for pizza. You can have both, and they have a few other menu items.

LOBSTER POT
321 Commercial St, Provincetown, 508-487-0842
www.ptownlobsterpot.com
CUISINE: Seafood
DRINKS: Full Bar
SERVING: Lunch and Dinner
PRICE RANGE: $$
Nice selection of raw bar items: oysters with sour cream and caviar; crab claw cocktail; lobster avocado cocktail, oysters and clams on the half shell. Main courses hit all the right hunger spots with baked Portuguese clams, Asian steamed littlenecks, lobster ravioli, blackened tuna sashimi, sautéed squid. Sit in

the unpretentious room and look out over the harbor. Spacious bar, outdoor deck.

LOCAL 186
186 Commercial St., Provincetown, 508-487-7555
www.local186.com
CUISINE: American; Burgers
DRINKS: Full Bar
SERVING: Daily lunch and dinner
PRICE RANGE: $$
Great burgers and beers. This place is always packed and open later than most of the other restaurants. There is plenty of indoor and outdoor seating.

MEWS RESTAURANT & CAFÉ
429 Commercial St., Provincetown, 508-487-1500
www.mews.com
CUISINE: American
DRINKS: Full Bar
SERVING: Daily dinner
PRICE RANGE: $$$
They call this place the Mews because it once was a stable where horses would cart oysters up from the bay to Commercial Street. The place is charming and quaint. Here their vodka list is longer than the wine list. They have a selection of 170+ vodkas, so be sure to order a Martini. They have quite an upscale menu: homemade chicken liver paté; Berkshire pork belly; fish tacos; a great burger with Stilton cheese; lobster risotto with butternut squash; lobster vindaloo; "shaking beef," a Vietnamese dish prepared in a wok, much more.

NAPI'S
7 Freeman St., Provincetown, 508-487-1145
www.napisptown.com
CUISINE: Seafood
DRINKS: Full Bar
SERVING: Dinner year round; lunch October - April
PRICE RANGE: $$
One of Provincetown's more unusual restaurants, it's located on a winding street full of colorful sunflowers and roses. It's a block away from town. Portuguese soup; Scottish smoked salmon; standout Bouillabaisse. For vegetarians they have a very good selection.

THE NOR'EAST BEER GARDEN
206 Commercial St., Provincetown, 508-487-2337
www.thenoreastbeergarden.com
CUISINE: American (New)
DRINKS: Full Bar
SERVING: Daily lunch and dinner
PRICE RANGE: $$
Craft beer and good bar food. They have 10 different brews on tap and 20 in bottles. Pet friendly in the patio area.

THE PATIO AMERICAN GRILL AND COCKTAIL BAR
328 Commercial St., Provincetown, 508-487-4003
www.ptownpatio.com
CUISINE: American; Seafood
DRINKS: Full Bar
SERVING: Daily lunch and dinner
PRICE RANGE: $$

Elegant and chic, they have a delicious inspired New England cuisine. Delicious raw bar with local oysters.

THE POINTE RESTAURANT
Crowne Pointe Inn & Spa
82 Bradford St., Provincetown, 508-487-2365/ 877-276-9631
www.provincetown-restaurant.com
CUISINE: American
DRINKS: Full Bar
SERVING: Tuesday – Sunday dinner, Monday closed
PRICE RANGE: $$$
They serve a seasonal menu with fresh ingredients. They seat about 50, making it an intimate experience. Bacon and deviled eggs; Buffalo chicken meatballs; lobster ravioli; poached lobster and chive gnocchi.

THE RED INN
15 Commercial St, Provincetown, 508-487-7334
www.theredinn.com
CUISINE: New American

DRINKS: Full bar; happy hour from 2:30 to 5; raw bar specials
SERVING: Lunch and dinner
PRICE RANGE: $$
This inn (from 1915) has a great restaurant: pan roasted local cod on a bed of rosemary potatoes and applewood bacon. The lamb chops are tops as well. The bar here makes a great place to grab a drink and absorb the atmosphere, or even better, enjoy the sunset.

RELISH
93 Commercial St, Provincetown, 508-487-8077
www.ptownrelish.com/
CUISINE: Bakery; deli
DRINKS: No booze
SERVING: Breakfast and lunch (till 3 weekdays, till 5 weekends).
PRICE RANGE: $$
Dozens of baked goods: double fudge brownies, chocolate dipped macaroons, triple chip cookies,

cupcakes, pies, you name it. They also have an excellent selection of delicious sandwiches for lunch.

ROSS' GRILL
237 Commercial St., Provincetown, 508-487-8878
https://rossgrillptown.com
CUISINE: American (Traditional)
DRINKS: Full Bar
SERVING: schedule varies depending on season; lunch, dinner
PRICE RANGE: $$$
It's the bistro on the second floor of Whaler's Wharf with amazing harbor views. They offer 75 different wines served by the glass. The seafood is fresh and well prepared. This is one of the few places on the Cape I've ever found cassoulet, so get that. There's also a 12 oz Porterhouse cut pork chop that's divine. Raw bar selections to start.

SAKI
258 Commercial St., Provincetown, 508-487-4870
www.sakiptown.com
CUISINE: Sushi, Asian Fusion
DRINKS: Full Bar
SERVING: April-January daily 5:30pm-10:30pm
PRICE RANGE: $$$
If you love sushi this is where to go. The space is amazing with high ceilings; used to be a Methodist church.

TIN PAN ALLEY
269 Commercial St, Provincetown, 508-487-1648
www.tinpanalleyptown.com

CUISINE: Seafood, American (New)
DRINKS: Full Bar
SERVING: Lunch & Dinner
PRICE RANGE: $$
Posh eatery in the center of P-town with a creative menu. Overlooks the ocean. Also has patio dining and a lounge (piano bar) with live entertainment from 9 p.m. Has a popular happy hour. Menu favorites include: Scallops with pea risotto and Swordfish with risotto.

VICTOR'S
175 Bradford St. Ext., Provincetown, 508-487-1777
www.victorsptown.com
CUISINE: American
DRINKS: Full Bar
SERVING: Daily dinner
PRICE RANGE: $$$
Delicious raw bar with a great selection of tapas. Enjoy the oysters, spring rolls, mushroom empanadas, fish tacos, meatballs, short ribs, and the sweet potato fries to name a few.

VORELLI'S
226 Commercial Street, Provincetown, 508-487-2778
www.vorellisrestaurant.com
CUISINE: Steakhouse
DRINKS: Full Bar
SERVING: Lunch and dinner
PRICE RANGE: $$
They have delicious Filet Mignon, Steak Diane, Rib-eye and Steak au Poivre. For seafood entrées you can find lobster, jumbo scallops and Wellfleet harbor

shellfish. They are known for their bloody Marys made with their own infused vodka.

WAYDOWNTOWN
265 Commercial St., Provincetown, 508-487-8800
www.waydowntownptown.com
CUISINE: American
DRINKS: Full Bar
SERVING: Monday – Saturday lunch and dinner, Sunday closed
PRICE RANGE: $$
They have an open-air kitchen serving multicultural foods. The bar offers signature drinks. Here they have live entertainment on the weekends.

Chapter 5
WHAT TO SEE & DO

DID YOU FIND AN INTERESTING PLACE?
If you discover a place you think I should check out on my next visit, drop me a line, will you? I'll mention your name if I end up listing it.
andrewdelaplaine@mac.com

ART'S DUNE TOURS
4 Standish Street, Provincetown, 508-487-1950
www.artsdunetours.com
There are miles of sand dunes near Provincetown and a real treat is going out there on one of Art's Dune

Tours. They'll show you the "artists' shacks" where people like Tennessee Williams and Eugene O'Neill went to work on their writing. (These shacks are still rented to artists.) In addition to daily tours of the dunes, Art's offers Race Point lighthouse tours and sunset tours that include a clambake served picnic style.

BEACHES

There are hundreds of beaches on Cape Cod, and everybody has a favorite one.

Among the ones we like:

Cape Cod National Seashore that runs for 40 miles from Chatham north to Provincetown. President Kennedy ordered it protected in 1961. It's idyllic.

Another great spot is **North Beach,** which is on a sandbar off Chatham, but you need a boat to get to it.

Race Point in Provincetown. You can often see whales from this beach.

Old Silver Beach in North Falmouth rolls out in a long crescent. Calm and quiet, but lots of families show up here.

Craigville Beach in Hyannis is also called **Muscle Beach** for obvious reasons. If you got it, here's where you flaunt it.

Nauset Beach in East Orleans is a grand beach. While here, be sure to get some fried seafood at **Liam's**, and don't forget their famous onion rings.

Sandy Neck Beach in West Barnstable and Sandwich runs 6 miles, featuring beautiful dunes and lots of birds.

Longnook Beach, Truro, **508-487-6983.** www.truro-ma.gov

<u>This is a beach favored by longtime P'town resident filmmaker John Waters.</u>
"The most beautiful beach, with this giant cliff," he says. "It looks like the credits to soap operas. It has real waves. Parking is nearly impossible, so I hitchhike there. I also just like hitchhiking. I have an old, handwritten sign that says 'Longnook' on one side and 'Provincetown' on the other. I get a ride in a second."

SUNSET (WHERE TO BE)
There are dozens of great places to watch the sun go down, somewhat of a "fun" thing to do out on the Cape.
Race Point Beach
Provincetown
Like a bunch of hippies in Key West, sunset-seekers applaud when the sun dips below the horizon here. (Yes, because of the unusual shape of the Outer Cape, the sun sets into the water, an oddity on the East Coast.)

Red Inn
Provincetown
An excellent place to watch the sun go down. Go before the crowds arrive so you can get a table and enjoy an early dinner.

DOG GONE SAILING CHARTERS
www.doggonesailingcharters.com
Provincetown Harbor Ferry Dock, 508-566-0410
Various sailing trips offered.

FISHING
Bay Lady II
9 MacMillan Pier, Provincetown, 508-487-9308
For larger parties or individual fishermen.
Ginny G
MacMillan Pier, Provincetown, 508-246-3656
Deep sea fishing.
Outer Cape Sportfishing
Provincetown, 508-740-4462
Capt. Jeff Duncan offers half-day or full-day charters.

FLYER'S BOAT SHOP & RENTAL
131 Commercial St, Provincetown, 508-487-0898
www.flyersboats.com
Here they have a boat called the **Long Point Shuttle** that takes you out to the very end of Cape Cod, Long Point. The Cape really does hook all the way around, completely enclosing P'town Harbor, thus making it the sheltered anchorage it is. At the very tip is Long Point Lighthouse. There are no roads, off-road tracks or trails to get there. It's a 3-mile hike if you want to do it on foot. Or, you can take a ride on one of their

boats to go see this isolated spot. It only takes a few minutes to get there by boat, and it's a lot of fun.

GALE FORCE BEACH MARKET & BIKE RENTALS
www.galeforcebikes.com
144 Bradford St Ext, Provincetown, 508–487–4849

KETTLE PONDS
So-called kettle ponds, or "kettle holes" were formed when glaciers retreated toward Canada during the last Ice Age. (Thoreau's Walden Pond is a kettle pond.) They make great places for fresh-water swims. There's **LONG POND** in South Yarmouth, located on Indian Memorial Drive off Station Ave. www.yarmouth.ma.us/index.aspx?NID=92.

Others are **GULL POND**, **FLAX POND** and **CLIFF POND**. Check out Jack's Boat rental where you can rent pedal boats, sea cycles, canoes, kayaks and the like on these ponds. http://jacksboatrental.com/ - Call Jack on 508-349-9808 for more. Rt. 6 at Cahoon Hollow Road and at Gull Pond, Wellfleet.

MARTHA'S VINEYARD / NANTUCKET FERRY
STEAMSHIP AUTHORITY
www.steamshipauthority.com
508-477-8600
Frequent daily departures aboard the Steamship Authority from Wood's Hole to Martha's Vineyard and from Hyannis to Nantucket. $50 round-trip; half for kids.

MASS AUDUBON WELLFLEET BAY WILDLIFE SANCTUARY
291 State Hwy Rt 6, South Wellfleet, 508-349-2615
www.massaudubon.org
In their 1,200 acres of salt marshes and pine forest, the good folks here offer bird and seal watching tours, as well as canoe trips.

PILGRIM MONUMENT
1 High Pole Hill Road, Provincetown, 508-487-1310
www.pilgrim-monument.org

If the pilgrims could see what's become of P'town, Cole Porter's lyric "Plymouth Rock would land on them" would come true. This museum commemorates the Mayflower Pilgrims' "first landing" in P'town and the writing of the Mayflower Compact.

PROVINCETOWN AQUASPORTS
333R Commercial St, Unit 1, Provincetown, 508-413-9563
www.ptownaquasports.com
Paddleboards and kayak rentals. At the Harborfront Landing building right on the beach just on the east side of the MacMillan pier where the ferries from Boston arrive. Their waterfront location is protected by the Provincetown Harbor breakwater. Lockers, beach gear, beverages, ice, paddling accessories, deluxe showroom, outdoor hot shower & foot wash.

PROVINCETOWN ART ASSOCIATION & MUSEUM
460 Commercial St, Provincetown, 508-487-1750
www.paam.org
Usually has moderately interesting exhibits. Good for a rainy day.

PROVINCETOWN TENNIS CLUB
288 Bradford St, Provincetown, 508-487-9574
www.provincetowntennis.org
5 Har-Tru Clay and 2 hard courts. Lessons, Round Robins & Clinics Daily. OPEN TO THE PUBLIC.
Months Open: Open 7 days a week May 15th - October 15th
Winter Hours: verify.

PROVINCETOWN THEATER
238 Bradford St., Provincetown, 508-487-7487
www.provincetowntheater.org
Always check their current production because you can't get any better theatre than they offer here. Building on the legacy of Tennessee Williams, Susan Glaspell and Eugene O'Neill, the Provincetown Theater is forging its own identity by promoting and sustaining the performing arts on the Outer Cape. Their state-of-the-art facility is active year-round, hosting or producing community based and professional theater, theater arts classes and a children's theater program. The Provincetown Theater has distinguished itself through collaboration with other arts organizations and its dedication to new works and local artists.

PTOWN BIKES
www.ptownbikes.com
42 Bradford St, Provincetown, 508-487-8735
They'll have what you need. Various packages.

SCHOOLHOUSE GALLERY
494 Commercial St, Provincetown, 508-487-4800
www.galleryschoolhouse.com
Thursday-Monday 11-5 & by appointment
The emphasis here is on promoting and exhibiting the work of some 50 Outer Cape and national artists in the fields of painting, photography and printmaking. The gallery takes its name from the old schoolhouse (built in 1844) in which it's located.

THEATRE
Cape Cod has a large number of theatres besides the Provincetown Theatre mentioned just above -- one in nearly every town as well as a number of festivals including the **Provincetown Fringe Festival** and **Eventide Arts Festival.** Check the local listings to see what's playing during your visit. You'll be amply rewarded.

VENTURE ATHLETICS KAYAK SHOP
www.capeboating.com
Whalers Wharf
237 Commercial St, Provincetown, 508-487-9442

WELLFLEET DRIVE-IN THEATRE
51 Rt 6, Wellfleet, 508-349-7176
www.wellfleetcinemas.com/drive-in-theatre
A blast from the past. But don't expect B or C movies. They offer first-run double features are all summer. If your kids have never been to a drive-in, show them what it was like.

WELLFLEET HARBOR ACTORS THEATER
2357 Old Route 6 Road, Wellfleet, 508-349-9428
www.what.org
They have a new $7 million stage named after longtime honorary board chairwoman Julie Harris. Top-notch professional theatre. See what's playing when you're on the Cape.

WHALE WATCHING
Whereas this area used to be the launching point for whalers to go to sea to kill the whales, now there are companies that will take you out to watch them.

Alpha Whale Watch
Provincetown, 508-221-5920
They can take up to 6 passengers at a time.
Cape Cod Whale Watch
239 Commercial St, Provincetown, 508-487-4079
Viking Princess Harbor Cruises
MacMillan Pier, Provincetown, 508-487-7323
SeaSalt Charters
MacMillan Pier, Provincetown, 508-444-2732
Though they really specialize in fishing trips (striped bass and bluefish), they'll do whale watching private charters.

Chapter 6
Nightlife

DID YOU FIND AN INTERESTING PLACE?
If you discover a place you think I should check out on my next visit, drop me a line, will you? I'll mention your name if I end up listing it.
andrewdelaplaine@mac.com

ATLANTIC HOUSE
4-6 Masonic Place, Provincetown, 508-487-3169
www.ahouse.com
Also known as the **A-House**, this place has been around for some 25 years. Locals as well as tourists comingle in this historic spot, which is oipen all year (the only dance club in P'town that is, I think). A good place to gather is the fireplace in **The Little Bar.** The other bar, **Macho Bar**, was the first leather and levi bar to open in P'town.

BOATSLIP TEA DANCE
161 Commercial St., Provincetown, 508-487-1669/ 877-ptownma
www.boatslipresort.com
An all-in-one resort is P'town's legendary Boatslip, with its 45 rooms (most on the water with a balcony). Free breakfast, parking available. It's the **Tea Dances**

here that put this place on the map. Pool with wide deck and a bar & grill. **Buoy Bar Lounge** is here.

GROTTA BAR
186 Commercial St., Provincetown, 508-487-7555
www.local186.com/grotta.html
The Grotta Bar at Local 186. Opens at 6pm. Has live entertainment, bands, DJs, a 46 inch plasma tv, a fireplace and cute bartenders. Martinis and signature cocktails and extensive wine list and diverse beers. Casual atmosphere with a speakeasy feel.

THE MONKEY BAR
149 Commercial St., Provincetown, 508-487-2879
No web site
While this is also a restaurant, it also has a lively bar scene with a big gay clientele.

PARAMOUNT
CROWN & ANCHOR
247 Commercial St., Provincetown, 508-487-1430
www.onlyatthecrown.com/paramount
P'town's largest nightclub on the waterfront with state of the art sound and lighting. Offers local and nationally recognized DJs. Hosts many important gay events, as well as the opening party for the Provincetown International Film Festival. Other events include fundraisers for local non-profits such as: Helping our Women, Outer Cape Health Services, the Aids Support Group of Cape Cod and many others. The most electrifying dance parties happen during Memorial Day weekend events in association with LesbianNightlife.com and

Provincetownforwomen.com

PORCHSIDE LOUNGE
GIFFORD HOUSE
9 Carver St., Provincetown, 508-487-0688
www.giffordhouse.com
Open year round daily 5PM-1AM. Includes: Martini Bar, Pool Table, Juke Box, Video Games, Fireplace and, in clement weather, their popular front porch. Lobby Piano Bar and seasonal sing-a-long 10PM-1AM, Friday-Monday. (The Gifford House makes a good place to stay, as well.)

POST OFFICE CAFÉ
303 Commercial St., Provincetown, 508-487-3892
www.postofficecabaret.com

The Post Office Cafe is notable not just for its pretty good food in the restaurant downstairs (a solid but not inspired wide-ranging American menu that will have a little something for everyone), but for its colorful cabaret upstairs that features pretty good acts almost every night of the week, including burlesque, comedy, and song. Good place to eat first and then move upstairs for the show.

SAGE LOUNGE
SAGE INN
336 Commercial St., Provincetown, 508-487-6424
www.sageinnptown.com
Pricey cocktails infused with herbs and fresh fruit plus small plates perfect for a light dinner or dessert with friends in an upmarket environment. Up the alley to 336-R Commercial Street.

SHIPWRECK LOUNGE
BRASS KEY GUESTHOUSE
10 Carver St, Provincetown, 508-487-9005
www.ptownlounge.com
The Shipwreck Lounge is an upscale and sophisticated space offering warm wood tones, a large fireplace and comfortable barrel chairs. It is the perfect spot for a drink and quiet conversation.

VAULT
CROWN & ANCHOR
247 Commercial St., Provincetown, 508-487-1430
www.onlyatthecrown.com/vault
Also at the Crown & Anchor is the Vault, often described as "what a leather bar should be." If you're

into the leather, uniform or bear scene, this is a definite must.

WAVE
CROWN & ANCHOR
247 Commercial St., Provincetown, 508-487-1430
www.onlyatthecrown.com/wave
Still another spot at the Crown & Anchor is the Wave Video Bar has always been a local hotspot and features resident VJ Tom Yaz with his "Retro Video Lounge" and popular "Stage & Screen Musical Night."

Chapter 7
SHOPPING & SERVICES

DID YOU FIND AN INTERESTING PLACE?
If you discover a place you think I should check out on my next visit, drop me a line, will you? I'll mention your name if I end up listing it.
andrewdelaplaine@mac.com

KITE STORE
277-A Commercial St, Provincetown, 508-487-6133
No website.
We're talking kites. More kites than you can imagine. The kids will love this place and, though you might not think you will, wait till you get here.

MAP
220 Commercial St, Provincetown, 508-487-4900
No website.
Sells clothes and gifts, books, odd jewelry, necklaces, belts, housewares. Attracts a very interesting crowd. (You'll see what I mean when you go in here.)

MUSSEL BEACH HEALTH CLUB
35 Bradford St., Provincetown, 508-487-0001
www.musselbeach.net

Open daily year-round.
Open since 1993, Mussel Beach Health Club has been recognized nationally by Out & About magazine, Cape Cod Life, and Time Out. Has over 7,500 sq. ft. and two stories of free weights, fitness machines, cardio equipment, aerobic and spinning studios, members enjoy a premier health club experience. Our group fitness program includes spinning, yoga, Pilates, bootcamps, boxing and more. Additional amenities include free parking, a climate controlled interior, and fully-equipped men's and women's locker rooms with showers, tanning booths, and saunas. Daily, weekly, monthly, seasonal, and annual memberships available, as well as discounts for guests of local inns. All memberships include full use of the health club, and unlimited fitness classes.

NORTHERN LIGHTS HAMMOCK SHOP
361c Commercial St, Provincetown, 727-344-6250
www.northernlightshammocks.com
Tiny little "shop in a shack" has everything you can imagine with the word "hammock" attached:

hammock stands, swing stands, hammock swing stand accessories, great totes, casual furniture, gongs and chimes, massage and comfort chairs.

OUTER CAPE KITES
277-A Commercial St, Provincetown, 508-487-6133
No website.
We're talking kites. More kites than you can imagine. The kids will love this place and, though you might not think you will, wait till you get here.

PROVINCETOWN BOOKSHOP
246 Commercial St, Provincetown, 508-487-0964
No website.
Filmmaker John Waters used to run this charming bookstore when he was a young man. And hey, it's a bookstore. Visit one while you can.

PROVINCETOWN GYM
81 Shank Painter Rd., Provincetown, 508-487-2776
www.ptowngym.com
Hours vary by season.
Open since 1976. Weekly rate and day passes. See web site for rates. Unlimited use, including classes.

SHELL SHOP
276 Commercial St, Provincetown, 508-487-1763
www.theshellshop.com
Blown glass, jewelry, starfish, specimen shells, large decorator shells, coral.

INDEX

A

A-House, 54
Alpha Whale Watch, 52
American (New), 39
ARNOLD'S LOBSTER & CLAM BAR, 27
ART'S DUNE TOURS, 42
ATLANTIC HOUSE, 54

B

Bay Lady II, 45
BAYSIDE BETSY'S, 28
BEACHES, 43
BOATSLIP TEA DANCE, 54
BRASS KEY GUESTHOUSE, 16, 57
BUBALA'S BY THE BAY, 28
Buoy Bar Lounge, 55
BUS SERVICE, 13

C

CANTEEN, 29
Cape Air, 13
Cape Cod National Seashore, 43
Cape Cod Whale Watch, 52
CAPE COLONY INN, 17
CAPTAIN'S HOUSE, 17

CARPE DIEM GUESTHOUSE & SPA, 17
Central House Restaurant, 19
CIRO & SAL'S, 29
CLIFF POND, 46
Craigville Beach, 43
CREW'S QUARTERS, 18
CROWN & ANCHOR, 55, 57, 58
CROWN & ANCHOR INN, 19
CROWNE POINTE, 19

D

DOG GONE SAILING CHARTERS, 45

F

FANIZZI'S BY THE SEA, 30
FERRY SERVICE, 13
Fish & Chips, 29
FISHING, 45
FLAX POND, 46
FLYER'S BOAT SHOP & RENTAL, 45
FOXBERRY INN, 20
FRONT STREET, 31

G

GALE FORCE BEACH MARKET & BIKE RENTALS, 11, 46
GIFFORD HOUSE, 21, 56
Ginny G, 45
GROTTA BAR, 55
GULL POND, 46

H

Hy-Line Cruises, 9

I

Island Queen, 9
Islands, 9
Italian, 29

J

JOHN DOUGH'S, 32

K

KETTLE PONDS, 46

L

LAND'S END INN, 22
Little Bar, 54
LOBSTER POT, 33
LOCAL 186, 34
Long Point Shuttle, 45
LONG POND, 46
Longnook Beach, 43
Lower Cape, 7

M

Macho Bar, 54
MAP, 59
Martha's Vineyard, 9
MARTHA'S VINEYARD, 47

MASS AUDUBON WELLFLEET BAY WILDLIFE SANCTUARY, 47
MEWS RESTAURANT & CAFÉ, 34
Mid-Cape, 7
MONKEY BAR, 55
Muscle Beach, 43
MUSSEL BEACH HEALTH CLUB, 59

N

Nantucket, 9
NANTUCKET FERRY, 47
NAPI'S, 35
Nauset Beach, 43
NOR'EAST BEER GARDEN, 35
North Beach, 43
NORTHERN LIGHTS HAMMOCK SHOP, 60

O

Old Silver Beach, 43
OUTER CAPE KITES, 61
Outer Cape Sportfishing, 45

P

Paramount, 19
PARAMOUNT, 55
PATIO AMERICAN GRILL AND COCKTAIL BAR, 35
Pied Piper, 9
PILGRIM MONUMENT, 47
POINTE RESTAURANT, 36
Pointe, The, 20
PORCHSIDE LOUNGE, 56
POST OFFICE CAFÉ, 56

PRINCE ALBERT GUEST HOUSE, 23
PROVINCETOWN AQUASPORTS, 48
PROVINCETOWN ART ASSOCIATION & MUSEUM, 48
PROVINCETOWN BOOKSHOP, 61
PROVINCETOWN GYM, 61
PROVINCETOWN TENNIS CLUB, 48
PROVINCETOWN THEATER, 49
PTOWN BIKES, 12, 49

R

Race Point, 43
RED INN, 36
RELISH, 37
ROSE ACRE, 24
ROSS' GRILL, 38

S

SAGE INN, 57
SAGE LOUNGE, 57
SAKI, 38
SANDCASTLE RESORT & CLUB, 24
Sandy Neck Beach, 43
SCHOOLHOUSE GALLERY, 49
Seafood, 29, 39
SeaSalt Charters, 52
SHELL SHOP, 62
Shipwreck Lounge, 17
SHIPWRECK LOUNGE, 57
Shui Spa, 20
Steamship Authority, 9

STEAMSHIP AUTHORITY, 47
SUNSET (WHERE TO BE), 44
SURFSIDE HOTEL AND SUITES, 25

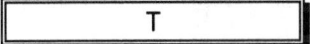
T

Tea Dances, 54
THEATRE, 50
TIN PAN ALLEY, 38

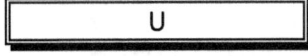
U

Upper Cape, 6

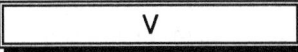
V

Vault, 19

VAULT, 57
VENTURE ATHLETICS KAYAK SHOP, 50
VICTOR'S, 39
Viking Princess Harbor Cruises, 52
VORELLI'S, 39

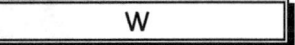
W

WAVE, 58
Wave Video Bar, 19
WAYDOWNTOWN, 40
WELLFLEET DRIVE-IN THEATRE, 51
WELLFLEET HARBOR ACTORS THEATER, 51
WHALE WATCHING, 51
WHITE PORCH INN, 25

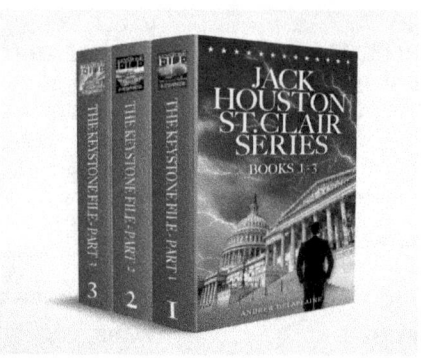

WANT 3 *FREE* THRILLERS?

Why, of course you do!
If you like these writers--
Vince Flynn, Brad Thor, Tom Clancy, James Patterson, David Baldacci, John Grisham, Brad Meltzer, Daniel Silva, Don DeLillo
If you like these TV series –
House of Cards, Scandal, West Wing, The Good Wife, Madam Secretary, Designated Survivor

> You'll love the **unputdownable** series about
> Jack Houston St. Clair, with political intrigue, romance,
> and loads of action and suspense.

Besides writing travel books, I've written political thrillers for many years that have delighted hundreds of thousands of readers. I want to introduce you to my work!
Send me an email and I'll send you a link where you can download the first 3 books in my bestselling series, absolutely FREE.

Mention **this book** when you email me.
andrewdelaplaine@mac.com

www.ingramcontent.com/pod-product-compliance
Lightning Source LLC
LaVergne TN
LVHW021622080426
835510LV00019B/2714